A Young Person's Guide to Lichtenbergianism

> Procrastination as a creative strategy!

by Dale Lyles

Georg Christoph Lichtenberg

A Young Person's Guide to
Lichtenbergianism

procrastination as a creative strategy

(or, How to make the Thing That Is Not)

by Dale Lyles

The Lichtenbergian Press

2024

Published by Lichtenbergian Press, an imprint of Boll Weevil Press.

bollweevilpress.com

Copyright © 2024 Dale Lyles

All rights reserved.

This book was designed by Dale Lyles. Text is set in Atkinson Hyperlegible. Captions are in American Typewriter. Quotes are in Designer Notes. Dingbats are in Skribblugh Extra.

ISBN-13: 978-7334670-4-9

to my scenius, the Lichtenbergians

Contents

Foreword 7
Introduction 11
Airport Version 28
Task Avoidance 39
Waste Books 47
Abortive Attempts 57
Gestalt 62
Successive Approximation 68
Ritual 77
Steal From The Best 92
Audience 99
Abandonment 105
Wrapping up 109
About the Author 110

Foreword

It took me nine months to write this foreword.

Duty always seems to come in times of creative inspiration. Or maybe it's the reverse; possibly the overwhelming nature of responsibility makes it all the more attractive to dive into our other worlds and create something entirely different than what's expected, and sometimes needed, of us.

A Spanish dramatist called Lorca described artistic inspiration as something called "Duende": a trouble-making Goblin on your shoulder. The Goblin doesn't care that the paper is due on Monday, or that your dad just asked you to do the dishes, or even that the author of a book is patiently waiting on your foreword (sorry), it appears on its own time, wreaks havoc, and leaves when it feels ignored or bored.

How to control a little artistic goblin running amok, creating chaos wherever it pleases, is a difficulty I do not (yet) have the answers to. Goblins do not like being told what to do. It's like being told you must sit at your desk and not move until you write ten pages. Suddenly, those pages become the most gigantic, drawn-out pages of your life.

So how do you make those pages come? How do you write a forward, or an essay, or a poem that has been stuck in your head for months

Young Person's Guide to Lichtenbergianism

when that Goblin is running around or has run away entirely?

I am many things, but my favorite is that I am an actor. When I had just been acting for a few years, Mr. Lyles was a teacher of mine in an acting summer camp. I love theatre for a whole lotta reasons, but at that age, I really liked to take a script and see how I could make it my own. After all, the words were given to me, so I never worried about what to say.

So when Mr. Lyles said we had to write our own monologues, my heart dropped. Suddenly writing, which I had always enjoyed but kept personal, was something I was showing other people. I had no one else's words to play with; now I had to play with my own. I was terrified one misstep and I'd prove myself a fraud, a failure, and be kicked out of all theatres for the rest of eternity.

What really happened was that Mr. Lyles came and sat with me. He taught me how to make a makeshift WASTE BOOK (which you will learn to make soon too) and told me, "write anything; even if you don't use it, even if it takes time away from something you will use, write the first thing in your head", and so I did. Suddenly one sentence turned into three, my first sentence was my closing line, and words were crossed out and changed, but I had a monologue.

Foreword

Lichtenbergianism will not make the Goblin go away, but rather give you the tools to go up to it and say, "how can we play together?". Creating can sometimes be as simple as writing a few sentences you never think you'll use. If you avoid making out of fear that you might do it wrong, you miss out on giving your Goblin the chance to do anything that might be right.

That said, procrastination is only a loss if you do nothing in the time that you're avoiding doing something. So if you have a Lego set you haven't built, a poem itching in your head, or a song you just can't forget, I invite you to consider avoiding those tasks with a book that will teach you how to create something from them. Art is a invigorating friend to have if you learn how to talk to it, and this book might just help you learn the right language.

—Molly McInturff, actress

10

Introduction

Hi!

Are you the weird kid?

Are you the one who likes to write stories, or poetry, or blogs; or who paints and draws or makes comic books or zines; or who likes to act or sing or dance; or who likes playing music or even writing music; or who writes their own apps or programs — or maybe all of the above?

Of course you are! That's why you picked this book up — or why someone gave it to you. You're the weird kid.

But...

You have doubts. You're not *sure* of what you're doing. Every time you start a project, it doesn't go right.

Or you just start a project and never get around to finishing it.

Or you just never start it at all.

You start to wonder:

Am I really creative?

Take this quiz to find out.

Young Person's Guide to Lichtenbergianism

Step 1: HOW TO TELL IF YOU ARE CREATIVE. TAKE THIS EASY QUIZ AND FIND OUT!

	YES	NO
• WHEN YOU WERE A LITTLE KID (OR EVEN NOW) DID YOU EVER SING SONGS? DID YOU MAKE UP SONGS?	☐	☐
• DID YOU DANCE AROUND YOUR ROOM OR BACK YARD?	☐	☐
• DID YOU MAKE UP STORIES FOR YOUR TOYS TO ACT OUT?	☐	☐
• DID YOU AND YOUR FRIENDS PRETEND TO BE ACTION HEROES OR YOUR FAVORITE CARTOON CHARACTERS?	☐	☐
• DID YOU EVER DRAW A PICTURE LIKE THIS?	☐	☐

If you didn't answer YES to **any** of these questions, you should probably put this book down, because you may be a dog or a houseplant and you cannot read.

Introduction

Yes, you are creative because humans are creative. We are *addicted* to MAKING THE THING THAT IS NOT.[1] We cannot help ourselves.

So yes, you are creative. Unless you are a dog or a houseplant.

What Is Lichtenbergianism?

Don't worry about that right now. We'll talk about it later.

Right now I want to talk about Wolfgang Amadeus Mozart. You probably know his name; I hope you know his music.[2]

This is a footnote. It means I have something extra to tell you at the bottom of the page. Sometimes it's fun, sometimes it's more information.

---

1. Think about it: where there wasn't a poem, now there is. Where there wasn't a song, now there is. Where there wasn't a painting or a drawing... You get the idea.

2. If you don't, what a grand adventure you have before you! Start with his wind concertos: clarinet, bassoon (my favorite), flute (2), French horn (4). You won't regret it. Search YouTube for "Mozart bassoon concerto" and go from there.

✂️ Young Person's Guide to Lichtenbergianism ✂️

Mozart was one of the few absolute geniuses that we humans have ever produced. This is just fact. You will not find anyone who will argue against this fact.

When he was five years old, he had his first public appearance performing in concert, on *both* the violin and the piano.

When he was eight, he wrote his first symphony.

When he was twelve, he wrote his first opera.

When he was 26, he got married against his father's wishes.

When he was 30, he wrote his most popular opera, *The Marriage of Figaro*.

When he was 36, he died.

Wolfgang Amadeus Mozart, 1756–1791

Everything we know about him indicates that the music came straight out of his head and onto the paper in one pure and perfect stream. He never seemed to stop to think what came next. He never seemed to go back to correct anything.

Time for a little music nerd talk.

Introduction

MUSIC NERD TALK:

When you write music for more than one instrument, you have to produce a score for the conductor to use which has all the instruments on one page, like this:

1 flute, 2 oboes, 2 clarinets, 2 horns, some violins, some violas, some cellos, a string bass or two...

...and then you have to copy out the parts for each instrument.[3]

---
3. Yes, in the old days, you literally had to hand-write every part. People made a living doing this. They were called *copyists*.

15

~~Young Person's Guide to Lichtenbergianism~~

Here's the score for a string quartet:

A string quartet has a first violin, a second violin, a viola, and a cello.

Stay with me — there's a point to this.

~~Introduction~~

We know for a fact that Mozart could write a string quartet in his head while riding in a coach, and then when he finally got to pen and paper he would write out the *parts* first, only later filling out the score. *Who does that kind of thing??*

A genius, that's who.[4]

Of course, Mozart's would have been handwritten. All his stuff would have been handwritten at its first performance. A printed version would come later, if at all.

---

4. Also, maybe a genius who liked showing off, like Mozart.

🖋 Young Person's Guide to Lichtenbergianism 🖋

AND WE DON'T HAVE TO DO THAT. And by "that" I mean we don't have to produce perfect work straight out of our heads, ever. That's not the way this creativity thing works.

For Real, What Is Lichtenbergianism?

Lichtenbergianism started as a joke. One day some friends and I were arguing online about music, and one of us posted a quote:

"To do the opposite is also a form of imitation."

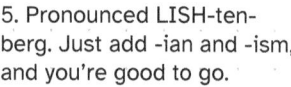

Georg Christoph Lichtenberg, 1743–1799

The author of this quote was Georg Christoph Lichtenberg,[5] an 18th-century physics professor in Germany. In fact, he was the first full-time physics professor anywhere. He did many cool things — we have printers because of his discoveries — but he *failed* to do many other things because he was always procrastinating. He simply put off doing the work!

Lichtenberg became our hero, because my friends and I were the same way. We had a *lot* of great ideas for stories and songs and

---

5. Pronounced LISH-tenberg. Just add -ian and -ism, and you're good to go.

Introduction

plays, and sometimes we would start on them, but we almost never finished them.[6]

So we formed The Lichtenbergian Society to celebrate the idea that procrastination was key to the creative process. No, it doesn't make sense. How can you be creative if you never get anything done? Mostly The Lichtenbergian Society was just an excuse to get together and hang out.

But after five years of getting together to celebrate our procrastination, we noticed a weird thing. All of us were doing *more* than we had before! Jeff was writing books — I was composing music — Mike was writing and starring in plays. How was this possible?

Here is part of the answer.[7]

---

6. Does this sound like you and your friends? Good!

7. The rest of this book is the rest of the answer.

19

𝓦𝓐 Young Person's Guide to Lichtenbergianism 𝓦𝓐

Imagine some guy, some random guy. We'll call them THAT GUY.

You choose: does THAT GUY want to write music or books?

If THAT GUY wants to write music, go to the next page.

If they want to write books, turn to p. 22.

✄ Introduction ✄

Imagine THAT GUY decides they want to write music, and THAT GUY decides to compare themselves to Mozart.

Faced with Mozart's fearsome perfection, THAT GUY decides they shouldn't even bother trying to write music. After all, they will *never* be as good as Mozart.

And they're right. They never will.[8]

Neither will you or I, but you and I know that we don't have to be. We only have to be as good as we can be. That's what this book is about. Memorize this: **Failure is always an option.**

Plus, who on earth compares themselves to Mozart? Don't be THAT GUY.

---

8. Especially if they never try.

Young Person's Guide to Lichtenbergianism

Imagine THAT GUY decides they want to write books, and THAT GUY decides to compare themselves to J.R.R. Tolkien.

Faced with Tolkien's incredible creation, THAT GUY decides they shouldn't even bother trying to write books. After all, they will *never* be as good as J.R.R. Tolkien.

And they're right. They never will.[9]

Neither will you or I, but you and I know that we don't have to be. We only have to be as good as we can be. That's what this book is about. Memorize this: **Failure is always an option.**

Plus, who on earth compares themselves to J.R.R. Tolkien? Don't be THAT GUY.

---

9. Especially if they never try.

Introduction

So why do we think we're "supposed" to be perfect like Mozart or J.R.R. Tolkien? Why do so many people say they are not "creative"?

These days it's mostly because we are surrounded by magic. Every movie or TV show we see, every song we hear, every book we read — they're *perfect*, aren't they? Just like THAT GUY, we think we cannot possibly do anything that good, and so we do not try.

We think you have to go to school to be an artist or a musician or a writer.[10]

We think you have to be a genius to be an artist or a musician or a writer.[11]

We think you have to be famous to be an artist or a musician or a writer.[12]

What do people say when offered a chance to create art? "Oh, I can't even draw a straight line."[13] We just don't think we can do it. We are all afraid of failure.

---

10. You don't.

11. You don't.

12. You don't. YOU'RE A KID, REMEMBER?

13. I have two answers to that: 1) No one's asking you to draw a straight line; and 2) If you need to draw a straight line, get a ruler.

Young Person's Guide to Lichtenbergianism

Try this. Copy this letter and mail it to your favorite author or singer or artist.[14] Go ahead. I'll wait.

> [Date]
>
> Dear [Your idol],
>
> I'm reading a book called Young Person's Guide to Lichtenbergianism and the author says that you fail sometimes when you're working on a new project.
>
> Is this true?
>
> Sincerely,
>
> [Signature]
> [Your address, so they can mail you back]

---

14. Or email or tweet. Whatever.

 Introduction

What was their answer? It was something like this, wasn't it?

> Dear [You],
>
> Are you crazy? I fail <u>all the time</u>. Everybody does. That's the way it works.
>
> Sincerely,
>
> [Your idol]
>
> P.S. <u>Young Person's Guide to Lichtenbergianism</u> sounds like a cool book. Where can I get one?

Don't confuse creativity with training.

Don't confuse creativity with "genius" (like Mozart/Tolkien).

Don't confuse creativity with fame.

Young Person's Guide to Lichtenbergianism

What Is A Precept?[15]

A precept is a general rule, a way to guide your behavior or your thinking.

We have nine Precepts. Each one is simple to understand and easy to put into practice.

1. TASK AVOIDANCE
2. WASTE BOOKS
3. ABORTIVE ATTEMPTS
4. GESTALT
5. SUCCESSIVE APPROXIMATION
6. RITUAL
7. STEAL FROM THE BEST
8. AUDIENCE
9. ABANDONMENT

That's just the list. Don't worry about getting them right now.

You don't do the Precepts "in order."

Precept #1 is not "more important" than #9.

They are all connected to each other, and each one has more than one meaning.

Taken together, they will give you *permission* to create without worrying about having to produce something "perfect."

Only Mozart can do that — and he's dead.

---

15. Pronounced: PREE-sept

~~///~~ Introduction ~~///~~

What I'll do in each chapter is explain the Precept and give some examples of how artists have used it in the past. I'll also give you some ways you can use it for your own creative work.

Ready?

But first…

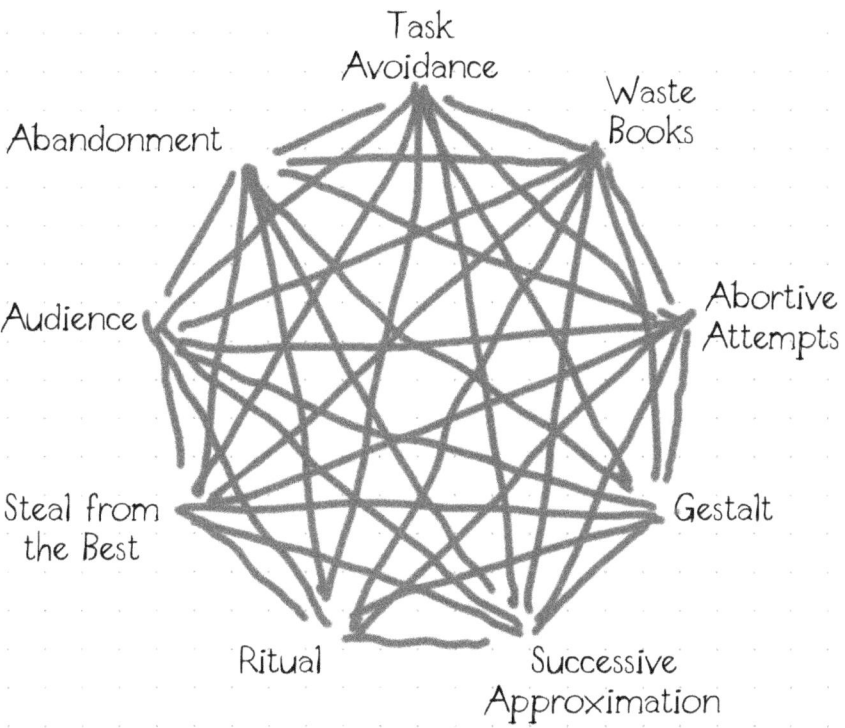

~~ Young Person's Guide to Lichtenbergianism ~~

Airport Version

In the "grown-up" version of this book, I started by giving the Airport Version[16]. That's simply a one-page description of each Precept in very basic terms. If you never read anything else, you'll have the basic structure of Lichtenbergianism.

You can skip it if you like. Come back to it later.[17]

---

16. When people are flying and are waiting to board their plane, they may decide to go to the bookstore in the terminal to get something to read on the flight. Usually you don't have a lot of time to browse, so you look for a quick way to see if you're going to like the book once you're trapped at 30,000 feet.

17. You will have noticed that the pages are printed with a gray dot grid, like a WASTE BOOK. *You can write in this book, and I encourage you to do so.* Scribble in the margins. Design better illustrations. Argue with me. Take my ideas further.

~~🖉~~ Airport Version ~~🖉~~

Framework

All human beings are creative: all humans are born to MAKE THE THING THAT IS NOT.

That means you, too.

Here: get started writing in your book by writing your name.

There. You've made your first mark. This is the way.

~~✂~~ Young Person's Guide to Lichtenbergianism ~~✂~~

1. Task Avoidance

Cras melior est: Tomorrow is better.

You can be more productive through procrastination by avoiding one project while working on another.

~~Airport Version~~

2. Waste Books

Always have a way to write down everything. Come back to it later.

Young Person's Guide to Lichtenbergianism

3. Abortive Attempts

Don't wait until you can do something perfectly before you begin.

Write "Abortive Attempts" at the top of your page to let the universe know that it cannot stop you from producing crap.

Produce crap.

Fix it later.

Have you been writing in this book?

~~✈~~ Airport Version ~~✈~~

4. GESTALT

GESTALT means "shape" in German.

Once you've started your ABORTIVE ATTEMPT, step back and see what shape it's in. What's missing?

5. Successive Approximation

Once you've assessed your project's Gestalt, tweak the project. Move it closer to being finished.

~~✈~~ Airport Version ~~✈~~

6. Ritual

Have a way to get your brain/soul/ear/eye/hand into working mode.

Create your time and space to create, then protect it.

~~Young Person's Guide to Lichtenbergianism~~

7. Steal from the Best

Use the past.

Reverse engineer the artists you admire.

~~Airport Version~~

8. Audience

You have two Audiences:

Those people out there

Those people right here

(And 3. Yourself)

9. Abandonment

Three kinds:

You can come back to it later.

It's ready for an AUDIENCE.

Failure is always an option.

Precept 1: Task Avoidance

When the grown-up version of this book was published every single person I knew made the same two jokes:

I do all my best work at the last minute.

I'll buy your book... later. (or I'll read your book... later.)

Every. Single. Person.

::sigh::

"Procrastination" means "to put off until later." It comes from two Latin words, *pro-* (for) and *cras* (tomorrow),[18] and usually people think of it as a bad habit.

It is true that if you have something important that you are supposed to do, it's not a very good idea to keep putting it off until you don't have enough time to do a good job on it. But that is not what we mean when we talk about Task Avoidance.[19]

What the Lichtenbergians are actually doing is called "structured procrastination." That

---

18. The motto of the Lichtenbergian Society is *Cras melior est* — Tomorrow is better.

19. I didn't even use the word "deadline" in the other book.

Young Person's Guide to Lichtenbergianism

means that we avoid working on one project by working on some other project. Instead of working on this book, for example, I could write a piece of music, or work on one of the other books I'm writing, or even go out into my back yard and mow the grass. Anything but work on *this* book.

The point is that no matter what I choose to avoid working on, I'm still working on *something*, and I'll still end up with this book, or a piece of music, or a freshly mowed lawn. Probably not today, of course.[20] But tomorrow. Maybe.

Believe it or not, this works.

One of the jokes the Lichtenbergian Society always makes about procrastination is that the world would be a better place if some artists had procrastinated longer before writing their bad poetry or releasing their bad rap video on YouTube. We joke that they should have spent more time *not* working on the project.

Here's the real talk about that joke — there's a step in the creative process called the *gestation period*.[21] In biology, the time between the fertilization of an egg and the new ani-

---

20. WARNING: surfing the web or dawdling on Facebook/Instagram does *not* count as TASK AVOIDANCE.

21. Pronounced: jess-STAY-shun (I'm giving you these pronunciations because whenever you hear someone mispronounce a word, it's because they learned it from reading and have never heard it. Now you can talk about all this without fear.)

✖️ Task Avoidance ✖️

mal's birth — say, baby bird[22] — is called the gestation period. From the outside, it doesn't look as if anything is happening, but on the inside the egg yolk is turning into a bird.[23]

The same thing happens to creative projects. After you start your project[24], you may get stuck. That's when you practice TASK AVOIDANCE. Work on something else for a while. Go for a walk. Bake some cookies. Clean your room.[25]

All that time — while you're brushing your teeth or riding your bike or daydreaming in class — your mind is still working on solutions to your problem, until one day you shout out "Aha!" in the middle of class and now everyone thinks you're a weird kid.[26]

That's gestation. Don't be afraid to leave your project alone for a while and then come back to it. Don't put your bad poetry out there before it's ready to be born.

---

22. Or velociraptor. Your call.

23. Or velociraptor. Technically, the yolk is feeding the developing bird, but you know what I mean.

24. see WASTED EFFORTS, p. 58

25. Your parents asked me to put that in there.

26. Unless they already thought you were a weird kid. You do you, babe.

✂ Young Person's Guide to Lichtenbergianism ✂

Let's talk about how to manage your TASK AVOIDANCE, because let's face it: if you just keep putting off all your work, tomorrow will *not* be better.

You want a system that's easy to use and simple to understand. It should keep you aware of what you have to do, but let *you* decide what to work on and what to avoid[27].

My favorite method is called *kanban*[28], and it's super simple. To do kanban you will need something like a whiteboard or a bulletin board — something that you can put where you can see it while you work, or at least where you can see it without having to dig it out.

---

27. Beware the pretty notebook systems that tempt you to decorate more than you make notes.

28. KAHN-BAHN — it's Japanese. (But most people I know say CAN-BAN anyway.)

~~Task Avoidance~~

You're going to divide the board into three parts and write these headings at the top:

TO DO	DOING	DONE

~~WA~~ Young Person's Guide to Lichtenbergianism ~~WA~~

Now you need a stack of sticky notes.

This is the hardest part of the entire process: doing the kanban dump. Think of *all the things* you have to do or want to do. Write each and every one on a sticky note. Put all those sticky notes on your whiteboard in the TO DO column. Every. Single. One.

The first time you do that, it's scary — so many things! But remember, you're going to procrastinate on most of them.

✂ Task Avoidance ✂

Here's how it works. You choose *no more than five* sticky notes to move over to the DOING column, and that's what you work on. (I'd start with only three at first and see how it goes.)

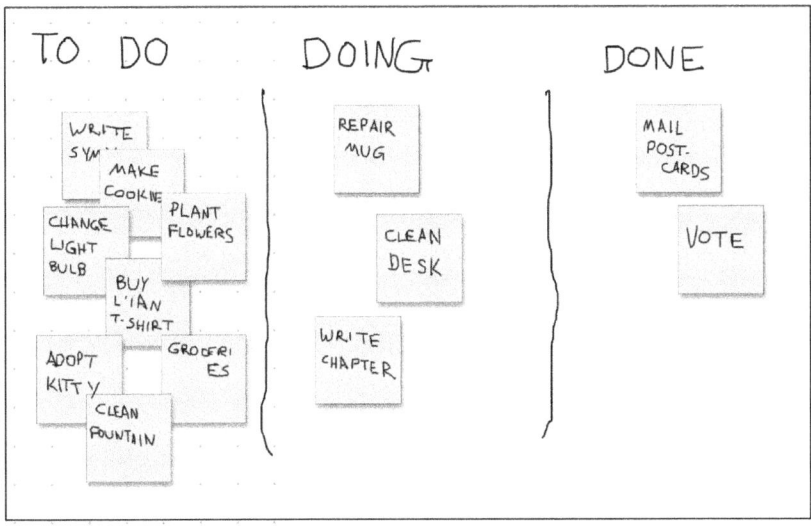

No more than five. If something in the TO DO column becomes so urgent that you have to work on it, then you have to move one of the DOING notes back into the TO DO column. No more than five.

When a project is finished, of course, move it to the DONE column. Personally, I just move them to the trash, but you may find it helpful to see what you've accomplished.

Young Person's Guide to Lichtenbergianism

When you do this for a while, you will start to notice what you *want* to work on and what you keep putting off — that's very helpful and will actually keep you moving towards a goal — or ABANDONMENT[29].

AND SO...

- Practice "structured procrastination" by alternating your projects — avoid working on one project by tinkering with another.
- Kanban your projects — know what you're putting off and why.
- Don't be afraid to let projects simmer.
- Learn the difference between TASK AVOIDANCE and ABANDONMENT.

---

29. see ABANDONMENT, p. 105

Precept 2: Waste Books

When I first decided to write this book, I pulled out a small notebook, slapped a label on it, and started scribbling.

You need a Waste Book. Here's why.

When Georg Christoph Lichtenberg was a college student, he noticed that merchants would scribble down the day's sales in crappy little notebooks — often scrap paper stitched together — and then would neatly transfer their scribbles to their actual account books later. He called these crappy little notebooks "waste books," and he started doing the same thing, only with ideas.

This is my Waste Book for Lichtenbergianism for Kids.

He always had a Waste Book with him, and he scribbled *everything* in it: ideas for experiments, witty sayings, letters he needed to write, shopping lists — *everything*.

He said that dumping all his ideas into a Waste Book was like throwing a bunch of seeds onto the ground. Some would sprout and bloom. Others never would. But, he said,

Young Person's Guide to Lichtenbergianism

you had to throw that handful of seed or you'd never get anything to grow.

It's a great idea. Every creative person — that's you — should have a WASTE BOOK and always have it with you. *Write it all down* and come back to it later. It doesn't matter if you're a writer, an artist, a composer, or a computer programmer: write it all down and come back to it later.

Remember Mozart and how perfect he was? Let's look at Beethoven, who was *not* perfect like that.

Ludwig van Beethoven, 1770–1757

Ludwig van Beethoven always carried a notebook with him, mostly because he was deaf the last half of his life and other people had to write their side of the conversation so he could read it. But as he took his walk every day, he would also scribble ideas for music in his notebooks. Not all of them turned out to be usable, of course, just like Lichtenberg's "seeds."

But if a melody kept bugging him, he would take it and write it in a *second* WASTE BOOK. There he would play with the idea. He would work on different harmonies or variations. He would figure out if it was a symphony or a sonata or something else. It always

Waste Books

took him a long time to work on his music.[30] (It was *ten years* after he scribbled down a theme that it finally premiered as his Ninth Symphony, one of his most famous works.)

Finally, if the piece *was* working, he'd transfer it to a *third* notebook, where he would actually write the piece. (He still made tons of mistakes. He was not Mozart.[31]

Beethoven's sketches for the Cello Sonata, Op. 69 — mostly mistakes!

---

30. Unlike Mozart!

31. And if Beethoven wasn't Mozart, why should we think we need to be?

Young Person's Guide to Lichtenbergianism

What are your options for a WASTE BOOK?

The most important thing to think about is that you have to be able to carry it around with you, which is why I like pocket-sized WASTE BOOKS. I know people who are never without their *book-sized* WASTE BOOK, but it means they always have to carry it or have a backpack or purse to put it in.

Other things to think about:
- Do you want to be able to tear pages out, or do you want something that will be a 'book' forever? (Both Lichtenberg and Beethoven kept all their notebooks their entire lives.)
- How many pages do you want? Do you want to have a single WASTE BOOK for the whole year? Each month? Each week? Each project?[32]
- Hard cover? Soft cover? Extra cover to protect it from wear and tear in your pocket?
- How expensive is your preferred method? There are some *really* nice notebooks out there, and that can get to be expensive. (Remember, though, that the notebooks that cost a little more may last longer than the cheap ones.)

---

32. I have a pocket WASTE BOOK for daily use, plus one for each major project I'm working on. Just like Beethoven.

✄ Waste Books ✄

Here's a neat trick that is fast, easy, and about as cheap as you can get for a WASTE BOOK. You'll end up with a small, disposable system that will let you—like Lichtenberg's merchants—scribble stuff down without worrying about perfection and then get it transferred to your permanent records.

Take a single sheet of paper, either letter or legal size.

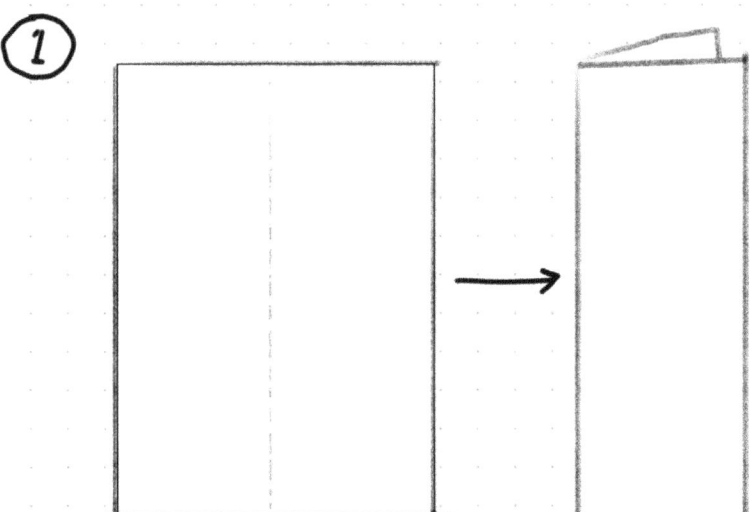

① Fold in half vertically ("hot dog style").

Unfold.

Young Person's Guide to Lichtenbergianism

②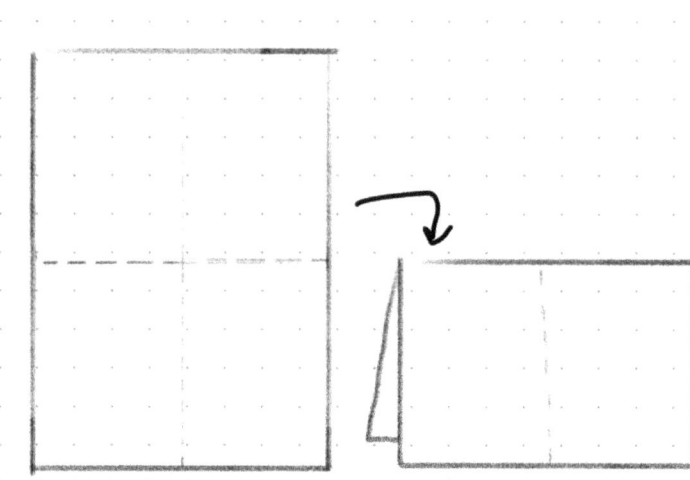

Fold in half horizontally ("taco style").

Leave it folded.

③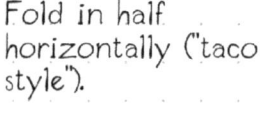

Fold both the front and back up to make a 'W' shape.

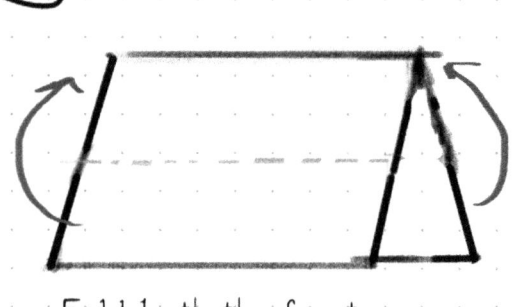

Waste Books

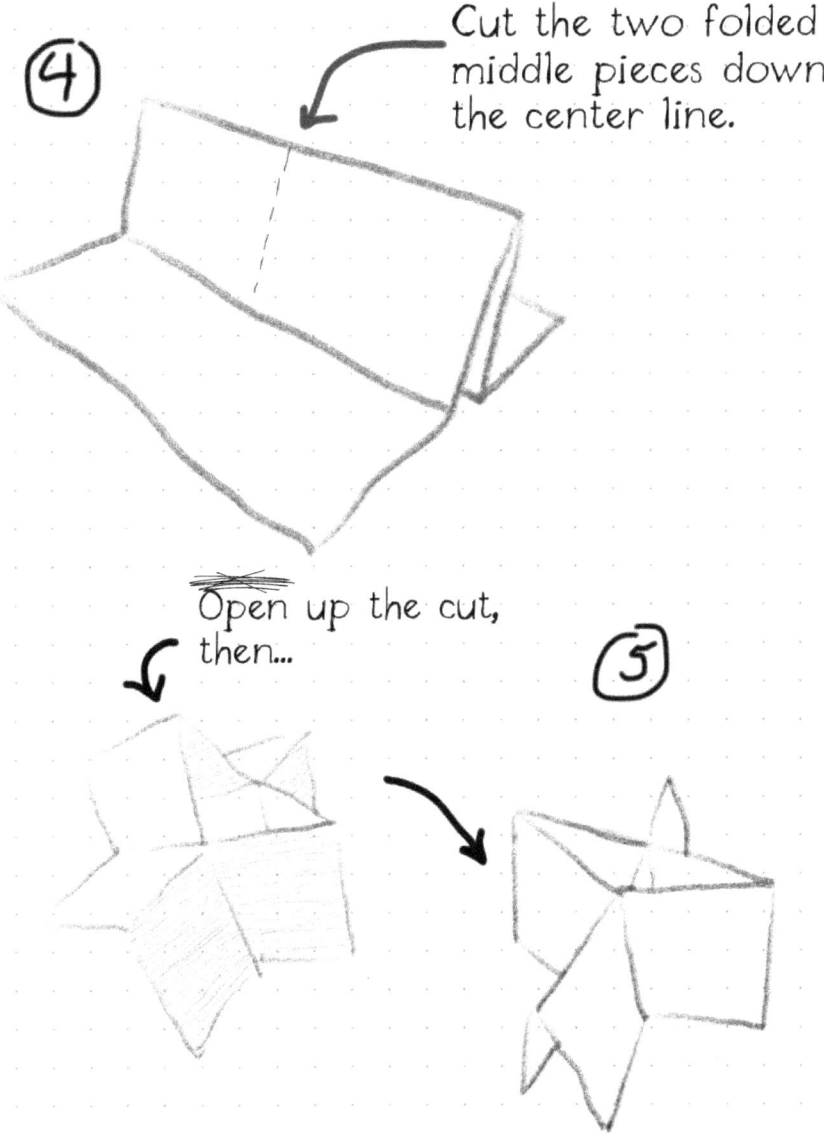

④ Cut the two folded middle pieces down the center line.

Open up the cut, then...

⑤

...collapse it all into a little cross.

✂️ Young Person's Guide to Lichtenbergianism ✂️

Fold it all up into your very own 8-page emergency Waste Book!

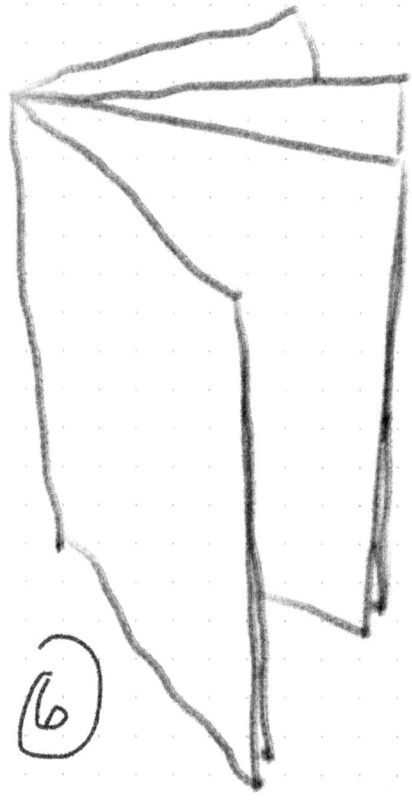

Very handy — you can use the clean side of any printed page as a recycling thing, and if you use a new, clean piece of paper, you can turn it inside out for another eight pages!

Waste Books

Let me say something about electronic WASTE BOOKS, i.e., apps for your phone/tablet. Because you live in the space future, you may prefer using something like Evernote or Notion or Bear to jot down all your ideas.

There are a lot of reasons why this can be a good idea: you don't have to carry around a paper and pencil; your ideas are readily transferable to your projects on your computer/tablet; your notes are always available to you rather than disappearing onto a shelf somewhere when your paper WASTE BOOK is full; it's easier to tag/label your notes and easier to sort and retrieve them.

If using an app works for you, then go for it. I have used a few in the past, but I have always come back to good old paper and pencil, and I'll tell you a couple of reasons why.

First, it is usually faster to use paper; by the time you've gotten out your phone, unlocked it, found and opened the app, created a new note, typed it in with your thumbs, and then saved it—I've already whipped out my WASTE BOOK, scribbled a note, and put it back in my pocket.

The second reason is that no matter how good the app is, you are always doing your work the way the *app* works, not necessarily the way *you* work. So as soon as you find yourself wishing

✂ Young Person's Guide to Lichtenbergianism ✂

you could do... whatever it is that the app won't do... then get yourself a good old-fashioned paper Waste Book and see if your thinking changes along with the way you write it down.

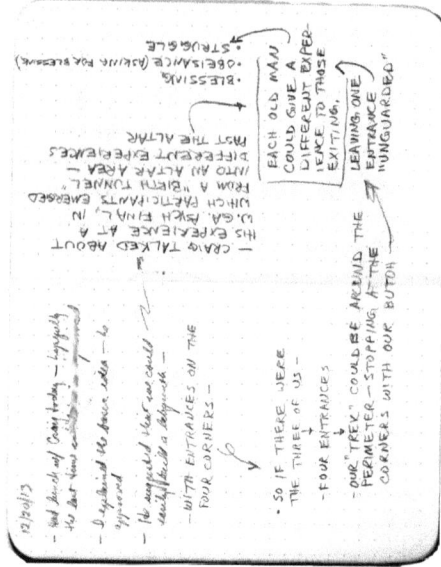

AND SO...

- Have a way you can record ideas and plans every day, immediately as they occur to you.
- Have a way to move these ideas into a framework of production.

Can your app do this?
If yes, then great!
If no, then try paper.

Precept 3: Abortive Attempts

What is an Abortive Attempt?

"Abortive" means "unsuccessful, failed, futile, useless."

Hold that thought.

The White Rabbit as herald, ill. by John Tenniel

Near the end of *Alice's Adventures in Wonderland*, Alice is on trial for some silly thing, and when the White Rabbit is unsure how to proceed with the evidence the King of Hearts tells him,

> "Begin at the beginning, and go on till you come to the end: then stop."

You may — most people do — think that successful/talented writers, painters, and musicians produce their works exactly like that: they start with the first (and perfect) sentence or line or chord, and then work smoothly from start to finish, whereupon they write THE END and everyone lives happily ever after.

No.

No, no, a thousand times no.

✏️ Young Person's Guide to Lichtenbergianism ✏️

Oh, it's possible — if you're Mozart. He could do it, but he was a freak.

We call this the KING OF HEARTS FALLACY,[33] and it's a trap. No one likes to make mistakes, and so because we can't see how we're going to do it without screwing it up, we never start our book or our drawing or our song.

(Or worse: you plop it out and think it *is* finished, without waiting to see if it is. (It almost never is.))

Now, however, since you're a Lichtenbergian, you don't have to fall into the Trap. Let me show you how to get started on any project.

It's easy: before you begin any project, especially one you're scared of messing up, write "ABORTIVE ATTEMPTS" at the top of your page. Go ahead and label it as an "unsuccessful, failed, or useless" attempt.[34]

What you're doing is telling the universe that you're going to screw this up and you're going to screw it up *bad*, and there's nothing the universe can do to force you to try to make it good. You're going to create trash. Lots and lots and *lots* of trash.

Wait, this is supposed to be a good thing? Yes, because you give yourself permission to fail, and if you have permission to fail it doesn't matter how you start. You just start.

---

33. A fallacy is a mistaken belief. (Pronounced: FAL (rhymes with Al)-uh-see)

34. You may also call it WASTED EFFORTS, which is the term that poet Nancy Willard used for her work. Or create your own term. Just give yourself permission to fail.

Abortive Attempts

The other part of the KING OF HEARTS FALLACY that keeps many people from starting is the idea that they have to start at the beginning and work their way to the end.

You do not have to start at the beginning and work your way to the end.

A Visit to William Blake's Inn, by Nancy Willard, won the Newbery Award in 1982.

The biggest piece of music I have ever written is *William Blake's Inn*, based on Nancy Willard's book *A Visit to William Blake's Inn*, sixteen poems set to music for full orchestra and chorus[35]. I did not start with the first poem at all. I started with "When We Come Home, Blake Calls for Fire," more than halfway through the book.

Then I worked on the other poems in no special order until I ended up with "Blake Leads a Walk on the Milky Way," which is the poem just before "Fire."

Not only that, but I didn't always finish a song before starting to work on anoth-

---

35. It is important to know that I had to get Ms. Willard's permission to use her copyrighted work to create my own "derivative work." This is *not* a case of STEAL FROM THE BEST.

Young Person's Guide to Lichtenbergianism

er one. I might have three or four unfinished songs going at the same time.

You can do this too. It's not cheating, it's not lazy, it's just the way the creative process works.[36]

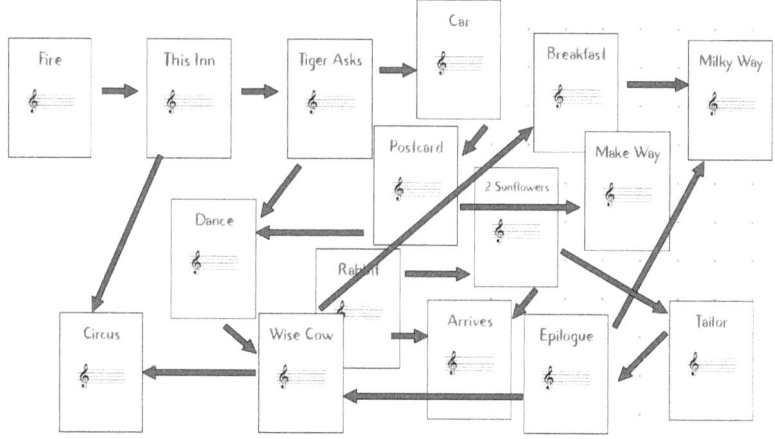

How I worked on William Blake's Inn. (artist's conception)

If you have an idea for a book, start anywhere. Start with the happy ending. Start with the big fight scene. You can even start with the opening.

Same thing with a piece of music, or a drawing. Start *anywhere*, and don't worry about making it good.

Do it wrong, and then fix it later. Don't wait until you can get it right before you start. Trust me on this one.

---

36. Don't believe me? Ask Lin-Manuel Miranda, the author/composer of the musical *Hamilton*. He actually wrote a letter to a friend asking if he needed to try to write the show in order, because he found himself jumping all over. His friend replied that he should just work on what interested him; the rest would come together as he needed it.

~~Abortive Attempts~~

AND SO...

- Give yourself permission to fail by labeling each page with Abortive Attempts.
- Deliberately set out to create crap — lots of crap.
- Plan if you must, but be aware that art has ideas of its own.
- You don't have to begin at the beginning.
- You can always go back and fix it. [Successive Approximation]

Or ask Johann Sebastian Bach why he wrote "J.J." at the top of every new piece of music. It stood for "Jesu Juva," Latin for "Jesus, help me." He had no idea what the piece of music would end up like and just prayed that it would be OK. (Given that this is J.S. Bach we're talking about, of course it was OK.)

PRECEPT 4:
GESTALT

So you've tricked your brain into creating a big pile of ABORTIVE ATTEMPTS, and all you've got for your work is a big pile of ABORTIVE ATTEMPTS. **Now what?**

It's time for GESTALT.

GESTALT is the German word for "shape." (It's pronounced geh-SHTAHLT.) In English, GESTALT means "the shape of the whole," and for our purposes we could call it **What's Wrong With This Picture?**

GESTALT is where you step back from your ABORTIVE ATTEMPT and try to imagine what it would look like if it were finished. It's like you have an image of your work, completed and perfect[37] — compare what you've got to that image. Can you tell what's different? **What's Wrong With This Picture?**

What would make it better? What do you need to change? Why is it *not* finished now?

---

37. It's not going to be perfect. Here's why: The brain isn't going to give you a perfect thing. It has a fuzzy idea, gets a dose of happy chemicals, goes "Great!" and hands it off to you. Then when the drawing or song or poem doesn't come out right, it says, "Oh yeah, forgot about that. You should fix it." We call that a *shinyperfect*. The brain is handing you an ABORTIVE ATTEMPT.

~~Gestalt~~

The difference(s) between your ABORTIVE AT-TEMPT and the "perfect" version will usually be one of these three things:

- NOT ENOUGH
- TOO MUCH
- OUT OF PLACE

NOT ENOUGH

- needs more cowbell
- more blue in that corner
- needs a cymbal crash at measure 83
- needs another verse before first entrance of the chorus
- repeat that section
- need more background for that one character before heading off into the woods
- got to find a rhyme for 'hat' that isn't lame

TOO MUCH

- too many syllables in that line of the poem
- too much red over the entire painting
- drop the violins, let the clarinets carry the melody
- that chapter doesn't move the story along
- does the dragon really need 18 arms?

Young Person's Guide to Lichtenbergianism

OUT OF PLACE
- need to fix the shape of the eyes
- wrong font for the poster
- move that piece of the newspaper collage
- use that chapter to open the book, then flash back
- that song doesn't belong in the show/on the album, so cut it
- her arm in the painting should be up, not down

Those last two illustrations are real. Broadway composers always write songs that eventually are cut from the show for making the show too long or slowing the show down or just not working. Recording artists are the same way. Every one of your favorite artists has left out more than they've shown you. As Georg Christoph Lichtenberg says,

"With many a work of a celebrated man I would rather read what he has crossed out than what he has let stand."

Gestalt

Portrait of Mme. Montessier,
Jean-August-Dominique Ingres
(1780–1867)

In another example, the painter Jean-August-Dominique Ingres did multiple sketches of Mme. Montessier before finally painting her portrait. Look at the sketch of her right arm (on your left). It's all over the place, and it looks as if Ingres had settled on having it relaxed down onto her skirt. But then when he painted it...

Fun fact (and you can look it up on Wikipedia): Ingres started this painting in 1844 and didn't finish it until 1856. Wonder what he was procrastinating on?

 Young Person's Guide to Lichtenbergianism

In other words, **What's Wrong With This Picture?** That's Gestalt.

The really hard part about this is that there is not just one "right" choice on how to move forward with your piece.

No wait, that's the *easy* part: there's not just one right way. Once you step back and ask yourself what's missing, the discoveries will come very quickly. The hard part is deciding *which* of the right ways you've discovered to choose. But that's the creative process — you choose one path, and keep moving.

Moving? Where?

[SEE: the next Precept.]

Here's a very good way to figure out what's missing from your Abortive Attempt: write it down.

Write a letter to someone famous to ask for their advice. Describe the problem so that even though they don't know who you are or what you're working on, they can understand the problems you're having. Ask them very specific questions about the problems. (You can even mail it if you like.)

Set a timer for two minutes and then in your Waste Book just write down everything that

~~Gestalt~~

comes into your head about your work. Ask questions. Be specific about what's bugging you, or the brick wall you keep running into, or the impossible choices you need to make.

Go for a walk. Enjoy the outside. Your body will thank you, and your brain will keep working on the problem. [SEE: Gestation, p. 40]

AND SO...

- Keep looking at the project to see what's not there — or what is there that doesn't need to be.
- The "shape" of the project will change — and that's OK.

~~#~~ Young Person's Guide to Lichtenbergianism ~~#~~

Precept 5: Successive Approximation

So GESTALT works like this:

Vague Idea of Perfect

We have a thing we want to make that looks sort of like this maybe? (See *shinyperfect* in the footnote on p. 62)

Successive Approximation

So we make our first ABORTIVE ATTEMPT.

Abortive Attempt

We compare it to our perfect image.

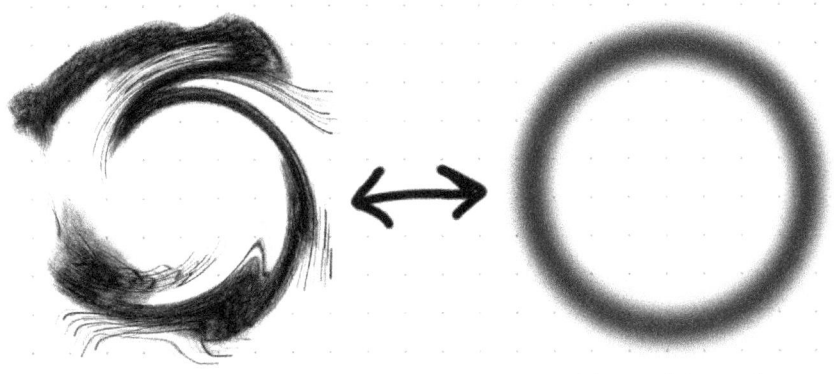

Abortive Attempt   Vague Idea of Perfect

Young Person's Guide to Lichtenbergianism

And that gives us some ideas...

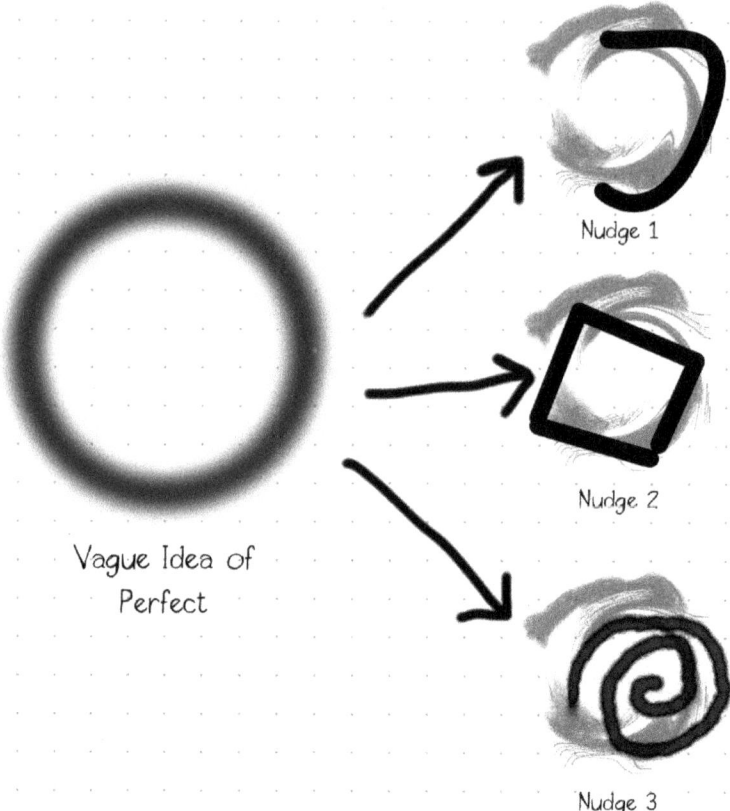

Successive Approximation

We choose one and go nudge it.

Nudge 1

Let's compare it to our perfect image...WAIT!

Nudge 1

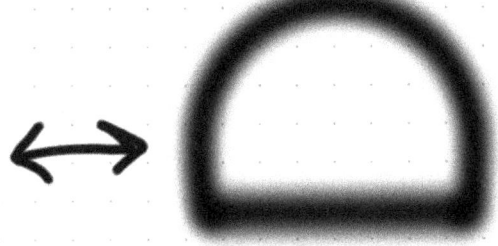

Vague Idea of Perfect

The perfect image changed! You can't do that, can you?

[sound cue: evil laughter]

Young Person's Guide to Lichtenbergianism

Oh yes — did I forget to mention that your vision of what your piece is "supposed" to look like will change?[38]

That's because every time you stand back to look at the piece and see changes you can make — those changes will give you more ideas for what your project may become.

This is SUCCESSIVE APPROXIMATION, which means that every successive change, you are not necessarily *finishing* the piece, only getting closer to the end. You are approximating each and every time.

Computer programmers do exactly this when they code, only they call it "iterative processes" — they run their code, then see where it fails or could be made better, and then they make the changes and run it again. At each iteration (repetition) the code gets better.

In other words, each SUCCESSIVE APPROXIMATION then becomes a new ABORTIVE ATTEMPT, which then needs a new GESTALT, which prompts another SUCCESSIVE APPROXIMATION, which becomes...

---

38. I did not forget to mention that. Go look at the last sentence of the last chapter.

~~Successive Approximation~~

Here, have a picture:

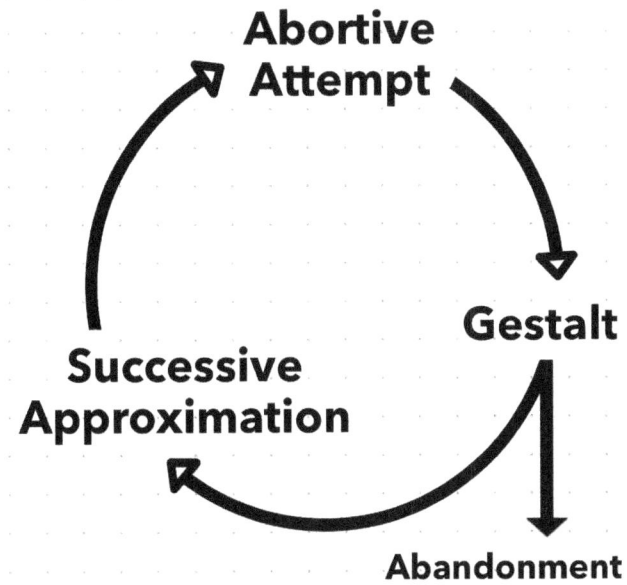

Don't worry — you're not stuck in that loop forever.[39] We MAKE THE THING THAT IS NOT by blundering our way through the cycle of "I'm gonna make some crap" — "Oh crap, it's crap." — "I'm gonna fix that crap" — until finally we get to the off-ramp and ABANDON our work to its AUDIENCE.

---

39. see ABANDONMENT, p. 105

~~Young Person's Guide to Lichtenbergianism~~

There is a very good book you should read some day if you are at all interested about becoming a better creator: *Art & Fear*, by David Bayles and Ted Orland. In it, the authors tell a story about a pottery teacher who split up his class, telling one half that their final grade would depend only on the *quantity* of their work, i.e., 50 pounds of pots would get them an A; and the other half that their grade would depend on the *quality* of one single pot they produced.

At the end of the semester, of course, it was the students who made *more* pots who ended up with the better work. Every mistake they made along the way was useful, either as a correction or as a new path.

It is like famous inventor Thomas Edison's statement that he hadn't failed 1000 times in inventing the light bulb, he had learned 999 ways not to do it. Each time you attempt a project and fail, you learn something new about the project.[40]

---

40. If you're paying attention. Pay attention.

Successive Approximation

Now that you're convinced that you don't have to produce a perfect work straight out of your head, have some Pro Tips for Successive Approximation:

When I'm writing and I'm going great in a sentence and then all of a sudden I can't think of the correct word or concept or person's name — I will just type or write XXX and keep going. The XXX makes it easy when I'm looking back over my writing to see where I gave up and left a blank.

Or when I have beginning and an ending, but not a middle, I'll put in an XXX for the missing section. (This book had *a lot* of XXX's in its evolution!)

If you can't figure out what comes next, *summarize* what comes next. "I need to connect section A to section B." "I need to explain the concept of the magic mailbox more clearly." "I need a better bridge between the chorus and the third verse."

Write yourself questions that you don't have answers to. "What emotion should this section attempt to express most clearly?" "What next step will leave me with different ways to move forward?" "Is there a way to embed Theme B in the music at this point?" "Should this section go in the chapter on Gestalt?"

Young Person's Guide to Lichtenbergianism

AND SO...

- The first version is not the finished product.
- Do it over, repeat with variations and improvements. Make it right-er. [GESTALT]
- Make it possible to update/upgrade the project.
- Don't wait until you can do it perfectly — dive in. [ABORTIVE ATTEMPTS]

Have you figured out that all the Precepts are connected to each other? You should write notes about that.

Precept 6: Ritual

This is the hardest chapter.

The Precept of Ritual is complicated and abstract, that is, mostly ideas and talk and not a lot of "how-to." I will try to give you enough "how-to" so you can make sense of it.

But first, some ideas and talk.

There's a thing called **The Hero's Journey**. It's a pattern that a man named Joseph Campbell noticed in stories of all kinds — myths, legends, fairy tales, even movies and novels.

Here's how it works. When the story starts, our hero is stuck in a yucky situation. Call it **Situation A**.

Situation A is not good. Your wicked stepmother has it in for you. The princess never smiles. You want to go to the Academy but Uncle Owen won't let you even though Biggs left last year. **Situation A** is yucky.

Young Person's Guide to Lichtenbergianism

To complete the yuckiness of **Situation A**, you — the Hero — are not quite a knight in shining armor. You're the youngest — you're an orphan — you're not very smart — that kind of thing.

But then something happens. You find a lamp. You give a glass of water to an old woman. The new droid runs off to find Ben Kenobi. Soon you find yourself going into the woods, or down the rabbit hole, or out to the Tusken wastelands.

You're leaving **Situation A** and heading into a completely different place: **Situation B**. This is the **Call to Adventure**.

yucky   adventure, struggle

Situation B is very different. It's scary, it's probably dark, and there are a lot of things you don't know and have never seen before. The **Call to Adventure** has dragged you into a **Quest**: slay the dragon, find a treasure, rescue the princess.

~~Ritual~~

Sometimes you get help from unexpected places — a dwarf, a wizard, Old Ben — but eventually you have to face the Monster at the End of the World. There you use whatever tools and gifts you've picked up along the way to defeat the Monster and achieve the goal of the **Quest**.

But you're not done yet. Now you have to leave **Situation B** and return to **Situation A**, only now you have the treasure/the sword/the princess. Before, you were a nobody. Now you're a hero, and you're home. **Situation A** is no longer yucky, so let's call it **Situation A2**.

A ⟶ B ⟶ A2

yucky   adventure, struggle   return, success

As you read this you may find yourself thinking, "Hey, this is just like Jack and the Beanstalk or *The Hunger Games*." You are right. It is.

Young Person's Guide to Lichtenbergianism

Now, finally, we're ready to talk about RITUAL.

RITUAL is a series of actions that are repeated in a certain order. RITUAL is designed to create a change in you or your AUDIENCE.

A worship service is a RITUAL.

Going to see a play or a movie is a RITUAL.

Reading a book is a RITUAL.

What do all of these have in common? They all create a space for our minds and our souls to work. And they all use the same shape to get us into that space and then out of that space.

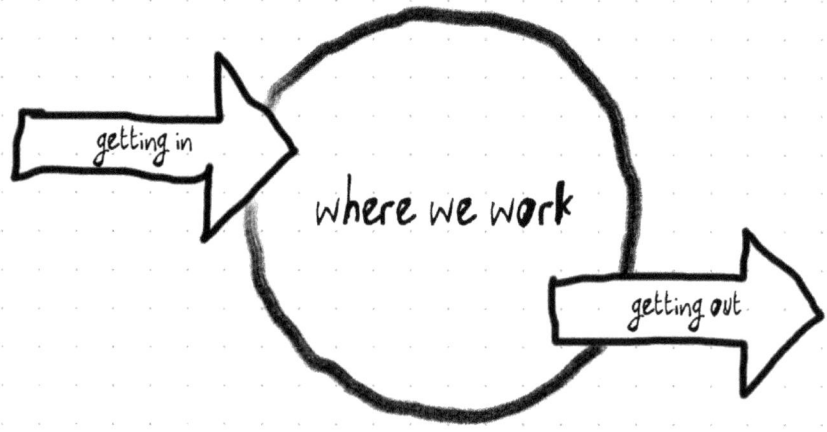

 Ritual

What do we mean by that? Here's a handy chart:

	Getting in	The Space	Getting out
Church/Temple	Call to worship	Sermon Music Worship	Benediction
Movie	Buying a ticket Finding a seat Previews	Entering the world of the movie	Credits Leaving theater Talking about it
Book	Being in a reading place, opening to bookmark	Being surrounded by the world of the characters	End of a chapter? Bed time?

You probably already recognize that the shape of RITUAL is the same as the **HERO'S JOURNEY**. Hold that thought.

MAKING THE THING THAT IS NOT is like the **HERO'S JOURNEY**. We start with an idea or some materials, and everything's crappy. We have to accept the **Call to Adventure** and head out into the unknown. We have to figure out how to beat our own Monster (our art) and then — if we're lucky — we get to come back with our new treasure.

Young Person's Guide to Lichtenbergianism

We use RITUAL to help us MAKE THE THING THAT IS NOT. Here are the terms I use to describe the separate steps of RITUAL:

- **Invocation**
- **Drawing the Circle**
- **Taking the Path**[41]
- **Breaking the circle**
- **Benediction**

Here's where they fit into our diagram:

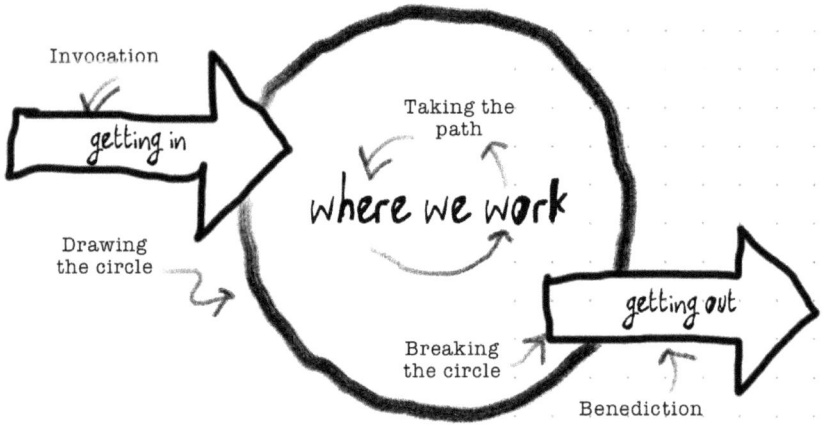

---

41. There's another step called *Numen/Connection*, but I've left it out to keep our discussion simple. If you're interested, you can read about it at http://bit.ly/LichtenbergianNumen

 Ritual

Invocation

To "invoke" something means to call upon it,[42] so an invocation is literally calling on... what?

In the RITUAL of a worship service, an invocation begins by calling on God to join the congregation.

In ancient poetry like the *Iliad* or the *Odyssey*, the poet would invoke the Muse to help him tell the story.

For Lichtenbergians, the **Invocation** means calling on our own creative impulses to MAKE THE THING THAT IS NOT. Art doesn't just happen; we have to *decide* to make it.

Sometimes artists make the decision to work at specific times every day, or on specific days. That's an **Invocation**.

When I whip out a new WASTE BOOK and slap a label on it for a project, that's an **Invocation**.

When you have an idea and can't wait to get to your art supplies or notebook or musical instrument, that's an **Invocation**.

The point is: You have to DECIDE to MAKE THE THING THAT IS NOT.

Then it's time to **Draw the Circle**.

---

42. The word comes from Latin, *in* + *vocare*, "to call in." That's what J.S. Bach was doing when he scribbled *J.J.* on his manuscripts.

✏️ *Young Person's Guide to Lichtenbergianism* ✏️

Drawing the Circle

In many ceremonies the leader will literally draw a circle around the RITUAL group. Sometimes it's a line scratched in the dirt, or chalk on the floor. Sometimes the leader will walk around the RITUAL space with a rattle or a drum or incense.

They are separating the ceremonial space from "reality." They are telling everyone there that they have crossed a boundary and left their normal space to enter a place where things will be—for a time—more special. (Remember the HERO'S JOURNEY?)

For us Lichtenbergians, **Drawing the Circle** means arranging our time/space so that we can get to work. We lay out our paints, we sharpen our pencils. We turn off our phones, block Twitter/Facebook/whatever the distraction might be. We put the Universe on notice that we're working here. Do not disturb.

Once you've **Drawn the Circle** and shut out the "real world," it's time to **Take the Path**.

84

☠ Ritual ☠

Taking the Path

In my back yard I have built a labyrinth.

Many people think a labyrinth is the same as a maze,[43] but we labyrinth fans say there is a difference: a maze is a puzzle that you have to solve, choices you have to make, choices that you can get wrong. Dead ends and failure are built into a maze.

A labyrinth, on the other hand, has only one path: once you start at the beginning, you cannot get lost—you just follow the path and you'll reach the center.

This is the pattern known as a 7-circuit labyrinth, because the path winds around the center seven times. A little research on the interwebs will give you instructions on how to draw one. Look for this little "seed" pattern:

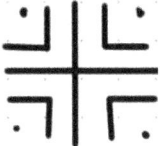

---

43. Mostly because of the movie *Labyrinth*.

~~✗✗~~ Young Person's Guide to Lichtenbergianism ~~✗✗~~

Here's my labyrinth:

Yes, it's as amazing as it looks.

Ritual

People use labyrinths for quiet meditation or thinking—remember that you don't have to think about where you're going—and so my buddies in the Lichtenbergian Society have a saying:

> Take the Path
> to explore
> uncover
> confront.
> Return to the Fire
> to confirm
> affirm
> retreat.[44]

So **Taking the Path** means doing the actual, scary work of exploring/uncovering/confronting all those ABORTIVE ATTEMPTS and GESTALTS and SUCCESSIVE APPROXIMATIONS.[45]

Just like the Hero, you have to get up and take that Path—you have to go into the woods—because that's the only way you're going to slay the dragon/win the princess/create art.

---

[44]. Does that sound like the HERO'S JOURNEY to you? Good, you're catching on.

[45]. You might think, now that you know about ABORTIVE ATTEMPTS—>GESTALT—>SUCCESSIVE APPROXIMATIONS, that the creative process is more like a maze than a labyrinth, with choices, dead ends, and failure written all over it. I will not disagree.

Young Person's Guide to Lichtenbergianism

Just remember:

Breaking the Circle

Eventually of course you have to Break the Circle. It's time to walk the dog, or do your homework, or maybe your brain just stops working.[46] It's time to quit.

But don't just quit. Take the time to say to yourself and to the Universe, "I'm done here. I'm going to be doing the ABANDONMENT thing for a while. Be right back."

Here's one weird trick that many famous writers use: Stop when the work is going great! Stop when you know *exactly* what comes next. That way, the next time you **Take the Path**, you're not staring at a blank wall. Not

---

46. It could happen.

 Ritual

only will you have the ideas you stopped with, your brain has been working on it between sessions. You'll be glad to get back to work.

So clean your brushes. Save your work. Tidy your desk.[47] Organize All The Things.

Take a step back.

Take a deep breath. Stretch.

Now go do your homework.

Benediction

Just as Invocation is as simple as turning the light switch on, Benediction is simply acknowledging that you're done.

In addition to turning the lights off, you should probably throw in a little gratitude there, as well as a promise to return. The Universe likes that kind of thing. Might make it easier next time.[48]

---

47. It could happen.

48. Spoiler alert: It will not make it easier.

Young Person's Guide to Lichtenbergianism

So, this RITUAL thing. You're probably saying, THAT'S TOO MUCH WORK or IT'S WEIRD.

It's not really. Remember:

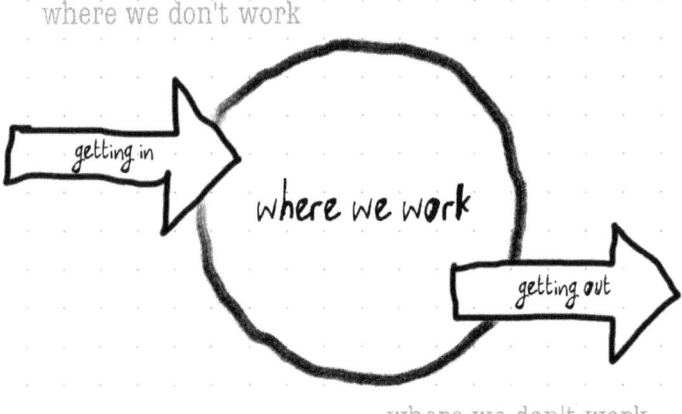

We use RITUAL to move from Where We Don't Work into the circle Where We Work. That's it.

Almost every creative person has RITUALS they use to get into that circle. Ernest Hemingway wrote standing up; Mark Twain wrote lying down. German poet Friedrich Schiller kept rotten apples in his desk. (He claimed that the smell helped trigger his creativity.) Some people write in the morning, others at night. Whatever.

 Ritual

All you and I need is time, space, materials, and commitment, and RITUAL can help us get all those things together. By recognizing that you're willing to get to work—**Invocation**, —you trigger your body/brain/soul to enter that space where the words or notes or ideas come from.

RITUAL doesn't guarantee success, of course. Sometimes you eat the Minotaur, sometimes the Minotaur eats you. But unless you enter the labyrinth—**Take the Path**—you will have a very hard time MAKING THE THING THAT IS NOT, and it's hard enough as it is.

Make it easier: draw that circle, take that path.

AND SO...

- Find the time and space that suits your working habits and needs, then protect them.
- Find a pattern that leads into (and out of) your creative space.

Young Person's Guide to Lichtenbergianism

Precept 7:
Steal From The Best

There's a saying among creative types:

"Good artists borrow; great artists steal."

What does that mean?

It means that we as artists hardly ever create something totally new. It means we get our ideas from everything and everyone around us. It means we learn from other artists.

It means we take from those who have come before and use their gift to us to create our own Thing That Is Not. It means we look at how nature makes things and we copy it. It means we understand the patterns and forms used by others and use them ourselves.

Just as Abortive Attempts lets you off the hook for having to create something perfect, Steal From the Best lets you off the hook for having to come up with something completely original. Because here's the truth: nothing is original.

Yes, of course every work of art is new and shows us something new about ourselves and our world, but nothing comes from nothing. Every artist gets ideas from other artists.

How does that work?

Steal from the Best

First of all, we can steal from the past. In the old days, that's what you were expected to do — there were forms you used, rules to follow, and you followed them.

At the beginning of the 19th century, though, artists and writers decided it was time to break the rules. (This is where we started getting the idea that everything had to be *new* and *original*.)

By the end of the 20th century, there were very few rules that artists *had* to follow, which may sound great — but absolute freedom can be really really alarming. Sometimes it's actually freeing to write a sonnet, or compose a sonata, or paint a traditional still life; those forms give you a path to follow, even if you end up leaving the path behind.[49]

So it's worth going back looking at these traditional forms, and using them for your work. You'll learn a lot about your art, and by learning the "rules" you'll know what you're doing when you break them.

---

49. **Take the Path** can turn into **Make the Path**!

Lichtenbergianism for Kids

If you're a poet...

- Learn the basic meters—iambic, trochaic, dactylic, anapestic—and practice writing in them.[50]
- Explore the old forms and rhyme schemes: quatrain, terza rima, sonnet, blank verse, etc.
- Write new lyrics for a popular song, or for a piece of music that has no lyrics.

If you're a composer...

- Explore traditional harmony; learn those chords and their inversions!
- What's a rondo? Sonata allegro form? ABA song structure? Find out.
- Write a song that mimics a song you admire: slow intro, big chord, rocking chorus, etc.

If you're a painter...

- Learn to paint a color wheel. Learn how to take a color from pure color to white and from pure color to black.
- Know how to draw the basic geometric solids—cube, sphere, cone, pyramid—and how to shade them.
- Study human anatomy and how all our pieces work together.

---

50. Pro tip: Work towards natural-sounding language. Don't reverse words in a sentence, and don't use "filler" words like *did* ("and so he did turn," that kind of thing).

~~//~~ Steal from the Best ~~//~~

If you're a _____

- _____
- _____
- _____
_____
_____
_____
_____

The second way to STEAL FROM THE BEST is to steal from artists you admire: Learn to play their music. Read their books. Study their paintings.

Reverse engineer their work. That means to look at their final, "perfect" product and figure out how they got there. Figure out what strategies they used, and then use those strategies to create your own work. As Austin Kleon says, "The great thing about dead or remote masters is that they can't refuse you as an apprentice... They left their lesson plans in their work."[51]

After all, I call myself a composer — I've written a lot of music — but I've never taken a class in composition. How did I learn all of it? I stole it: I stole it from textbooks and encyclopedias and album covers. I stole it from choral directors. I stole it from Mozart and Beethoven and Philip Glass.

You can, too.

---

51. *Steal Like an Artist*, p. 17

Young Person's Guide to Lichtenbergianism

Other places you can STEAL FROM THE BEST:

Steal from your culture:

Look at local folk art. Listen to family stories. Do you belong to a group or culture that has a definite "insider" feel? What does it take to be on the "inside"? What would mark you as an "outsider"?

Steal from the world at large:

The world has a gazillion different cultures around the world, and you can learn from any of them. For example, one of Pablo Picasso's first megahit paintings was *Demoiselles d'Avignon*, and one of the reasons it created a sensation was Picasso's "theft" of the geometric patterns of African tribal masks.

A word of caution here: there is today some concern about "cultural appropriation," which means that some people think it shows disrespect for one culture to "steal" another culture's imagery, music, costume, etc. Certainly if you are snagging something that has a religious significance in someone else's culture just to put on a t-shirt, that's not just wrong, it's cheesy. But it is my belief that we — human beings — are all in this together, and that if China wants to learn to play the violin and play Mozart, why should we jealously guard that?

Steal from the Best

Steal from nature:

In 1941, an engineer in Switzerland named George de Mestral went for a walk with his dog. He noticed that burdock seeds would stick to his coat and his dog's fur; he was curious about how they did that, and when he examined the seeds saw they were covered with tiny little hooks. Hm, he said, that could be useful, and he invented Velcro®.

Beethoven loved to go for long walks in the country, and his Sixth Symphony, "Pastorale," uses sounds and feelings from those walks — birdsong, peasant music, thunderstorms — as the building blocks for the entire work. (Many other composers have used birdsong as inspiration: Antonio Vivaldi, Olivier Messaien, and Ottorino Respighi among them.)

Beatrix Potter wanted to be a scientific illustrator. She was particularly adept at drawing types of fungus, but the scientific community rejected her because she was a woman. (Ironically, mycologists still use her illustrations of fungi.) She used her powers of observation and her gifts as an artist to write and illustrate children's books: *The Tale of Peter Rabbit* for starters.

You, too, can and should pay attention to the natural world around you.

✂ Young Person's Guide to Lichtenbergianism ✂

AND SO...

- Don't be afraid to emulate your heroes.
- Stuck? Look for how others have solved it — and try it yourself.
- Learn and use the great forms of the past.

Precept 8: Audience

As an artist, you want other people to see the THING you've MADE — you want them to see it, to like it, to appreciate it, maybe even give you money for it. As a friend of mine says, his paintings aren't really finished until someone buys them and takes them home.[52]

It's probably true that we'd all love to be best-selling authors/artists/songwriters, but think of this: Are there popular movies you don't care about seeing? Books you wouldn't read? Music you won't listen to? That's OK — all that means is that you are not the AUDIENCE for those artists.

The reverse of this is true, too: not everyone out there is *your* AUDIENCE.

So who is your AUDIENCE?

---

52. Or, he always adds, until he's dead.

✂ Young Person's Guide to Lichtenbergianism ✂

First of all, let me be clear about who your Audience is *not*: the Museum of Modern Art [MOMA] is not your Audience. The New York Times bestseller list is not your Audience. The Tony Awards Committee is not your Audience. You are not Making the Thing That Is Not for those guys.

In fact, even if you *are* on the NYT bestseller list, you are not Making the Thing That Is Not for those guys. You are Making the Thing That Is Not for *your* Audience.

Austin Kleon, author of *Steal Like an Artist*, said in a tweet one day something like: Imagine yourself appearing before an adoring crowd of hundreds, even thousands of fans. Do you imagine that every single one of them really, truly cares about your work? No, of course not. Maybe a handful do. Those people are your Audience.

I would add: The rest of them are The Crowd.

Don't create for The Crowd. Create for your Audience.

> Create for your ***audience***.
>
> Create for ***your*** audience.
>
> Create ***for*** your audience.
>
> ***Create*** for your audience.

Audience

You actually have at least two AUDIENCES:

1. Those people out there.
2. Those people right here.

That first AUDIENCE is that great invisible crowd of people to whom you will eventually Abandon your work. They are the ones who will read your book, listen to your music, stroll your garden, review your research. If there are enough of them, they may very well propel you to that bestseller list or that Tony Award, but even so they are not infinite in number. You are not MAKING THE THING THAT IS NOT for everyone.

Let me say that again: your work is not for everyone. It is for *your* AUDIENCE. Even our top earners know this. George R. R. Martin[53] is writing his books for readers who like huge, sprawling fantasies with hundreds of characters and a lot of violence. If you don't like that kind of thing, he's not writing for you. And trust me, he's OK with that.

---

54. Author of *The Game of Thrones*, which you probably already knew

Young Person's Guide to Lichtenbergianism

Then there's your second AUDIENCE, "those people right here."

If you look at history, you'll find that all the cool kids seemed to know each other. The artists, writers, scientists, composers of any great period partied together, shared studios, wrote letters, stole from each other, supported each other, argued with each other.

There's a word for that: *scenius*.[54] Musician Brian Eno made that word up by combining "scene" and "genius" — a group intelligence that results from all the cool kids hanging out together.

Who is your scenius? MAKING THE THING THAT IS NOT is just easier when you have people who are interested in seeing you succeed.

Do you have a writers' group? A band? A drama club? Here's a scary idea: if you don't have one, make one. Form a club at school. Start a band.

Start with one or two friends. Meet often. Share lots. Embrace difference!

Show interest in each other's work. Give feedback; criticize but don't silence. Express praise. Offer encouragement. Promote each other's work.

Form your own Lichtenbergian Society.

---

54. Pronounced: SEEN-yus

Audience

You have a third AUDIENCE: yourself.

Think about it: as you work through the cycle of ABORTIVE ATTEMPTS, GESTALT, and SUCCESSIVE APPROXIMATION, you are trying to please your eye, your ear, your sense of wholeness and completion. Only you can decide when it's time to ABANDON the work.

Once again, MOMA is not your AUDIENCE. None of the artists whom you admire, not even the ones who are filthy rich, create their work for some abstract notion of fame. It is certainly true that Those People Out There will give you money for your work — I will have no objections if this book sells a million copies — but the surest way to short-circuit your process is to stop listening to you inner AUDIENCE and try to hear instead the fickle and nonexistent voice of The Crowd.

Stick to your inner AUDIENCE; if it also pleases MOMA or the bestseller list, that's great (remember to invite me to your private Caribbean island for a stay) but never pursue an AUDIENCE that does not exist.

Most artists are in fact their own toughest AUDIENCE. Even today when I hear some of my music, I can hear all the compromises, the band-aids, and the outright failures to achieve what I thought I wanted from the piece — but almost no one else can.

The trick is to be your own AUDIENCE, not your own Critic. There is a difference.

~~Young Person's Guide to Lichtenbergianism~~

AND SO...

- MOMA is not your Audience.
- Find or create your scenius.
- Be your own Audience: journal your efforts in some way.

Precept 9: Abandonment

Remember the ABORTIVE ATTEMPT cycle?

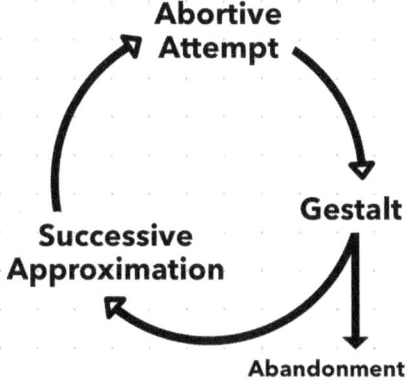

ABANDONMENT is the exit ramp off that loop.

Just like AUDIENCE, there are three different kinds of ABANDONMENT.

Young Person's Guide to Lichtenbergianism

Let's look at the hard version of ABANDONMENT first and get it out of the way: **ABANDONMENT = Failure**.

Lichtenbergians have two mottos: "Cras melior est" and "Failure is always an option."

That sounds terrible, but let me explain why it's not.

"Failure is always an option" is a great way to think about your work. Like the whole structure of Lichtenbergianism — of this book — the idea of embracing failure is a joking way to give you the tools to fail, to fail often, and to fail upwards.

The thing is, failure is part of the process. You may think that "failure" means that you did something bad, that if you were a *real* artist you would have ridden that wave all the way to the shore and then shaken the water out of your hair in slow motion like some golden surfer dude.

This is nonsense. You have not "failed," you have ABANDONED work that is no longer your work. *Real* artists know this. Remember, not all baby sea turtles make it. Not all art gets finished.

No, it's not fun. Yes, it's painful. But ABANDONING your work doesn't make you less of an artist, it makes you more of one.

Abandonment

There are two other versions of ABANDONMENT. The first is our old friend TASK AVOIDANCE: you just set a project aside and don't work on it for a while.[55] Come back to it later when you have a better grip on how to finish it.

In fact, even if you think a project is a failure, don't throw it out. When bestselling author Stephen King was young, married, and poor, he was trying to make money by selling short stories to magazines. One day he wrote an ABORTIVE ATTEMPT of a story, and it was so terrible that he threw it in the trash. When his wife got home from work, she found it in the trash and read it. She convinced him it wasn't terrible. She said it was good enough to keep working on, so he did. But it soon became too long to be a short story, so he kept writing until it turned into his first novel, *Carrie*.

So keep all your "failures." You never know when they might be ready to come back to life.

The third kind of ABANDONMENT is actually far scarier than failure, and it's when your project is finished and you have to hand it over to an AUDIENCE. As the French poet Paul Valery said, "A poem is never finished, merely abandoned."

---

55. see Gestation, p. 40 [in TASK AVOIDANCE[

Young Person's Guide to Lichtenbergianism

What did he mean by that? Sending your art to an AUDIENCE is like when you finish a project for school and turn it in for the teacher to grade. Will your teacher notice all the errors or will they think it's a pretty good job?[56] Likewise, will your AUDIENCE love what you've done, or will they hate it? Or worst of all, will they ignore it?

You can't be afraid of any of that.[57] ABANDONMENT is where you get off the ABORTIVE ATTEMPTS circle. The artist Pierre Bonnard was obsessed with perfecting the colors in his paintings, and the story is told that he convinced his friend Éduard Vuillard to distract the guards in a museum so he could touch up one of his paintings *hanging in that museum*. Don't be that guy.

AND SO...

- Give yourself permission to stop — it's OK to stop gnawing at it.
- Let it go — walk away from it and come back later to look at it. [GESTALT]
- Failure is a perfectly acceptable option.
- Be interested in your failures. Make them interesting.
- It's also perfectly acceptable to succeed.

---

56. Of course, it's your teacher's job to notice the errors. School is nothing more than the whole ABORTIVE ATTEMPTS cycle, and your teacher is there to help you with the GESTALT of learning.

57. You can actually even be afraid of stunning success, because what if the *next* thing you make SUCKS??

Wrapping up

And that's it: Lichtenbergianism, procrastination as a creative strategy. Now that you've seen the Precepts, you may be thinking, "This is the worst book on creativity ever — it didn't even tell me how to make my art perfect!"

No, it did not. It did something better.

If you are like me — and like most of the people I've worked with — the only thing stopping you from accomplishing your work is the fear that it's not going to be perfect. Lichtenbergianism shows you that it's not going to be perfect, and that's okay.

As I said in Chapter One, what I get out of Lichtenbergianism is the sense that I have permission to create, and to create crap. Because of the way the creative process works, I have gotten better at all the things I've created by creating more things, from writing to designing to composition to computer programming; that's the way it works.

Start where you are.

Use what you have.

Do what you can.

MAKE THE THING THAT IS NOT.

And then do it again.

Better.

Young Person's Guide to Lichtenbergianism

ABOUT THE AUTHOR

So who am I anyway?

I was a school media specialist for many years, both at the high school and the elementary levels. I worked hard to make the book collection in my libraries be the kind of library I wanted as a kid, and I've tried to make this book a book that I would have liked when I was a kid.

I was also the artistic director of our community theatre, and I worked with the Georgia Governor's Honors Program (a summer program for gifted and talented high school students) for nearly 30 years.

I've done a lot of creative stuff in my life. I have acted, directed, composed music, painted and drawn and sculpted, written poetry, blogged, written books, and programmed computers. I made a labyrinth in my back yard. I have taught other people how to do these things. And I've done all these things mostly because nobody ever told me not to. I hope you will do the same.

My website is lichtenbergianism.com

You can follow me on Mastodon @Lichtenbergian

Image credits: All images not listed here were created by me.

images on pp. 14, 18, 48, 57, 59, and 65 are from WikiCommons

Beethoven's score, p. 49, is from Beethoven-Haus Bonn

Wrapping Up

Look — blank pages!

~~Young Person's Guide to Lichtenbergianism~~

Wrapping Up

~~✗~~ Young Person's Guide to Lichtenbergianism ~~✗~~

Wrapping Up

~~Young Person's Guide to Lichtenbergianism~~

Wrapping Up

~~Young Person's Guide to Lichtenbergianism~~

Wrapping Up

~~✏️~~ Young Person's Guide to Lichtenbergianism ~~✏️~~

Wrapping Up

Go! Make the thing!

Are you a creative genius? No, only Mozart is a creative genius, and you are not him. But you are creative – – yes, you are, admit it – – and you want to overcome your fears and your bad habits so that you can write that novel/paint that painting/compose that song/program that app.

A Young Person's Guide to Lichtenbergianism gives you nine Precepts, ways to restructure your thinking about how you create and why so that you can just get to work and create the work of your dreams. But not today. Tomorrow is better.

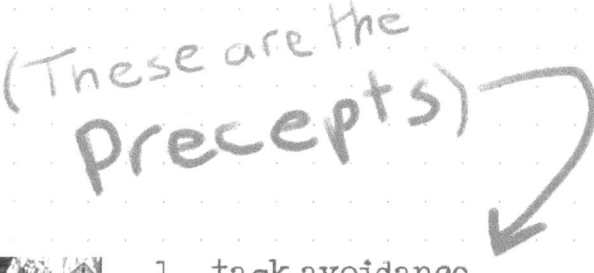
(These are the Precepts)

Author Dale Lyles has been an educator, a director, a composer, a writer, and more during his long career. He lives in Newnan, GA, with his Lovely First Wife.

1. task avoidance
2. waste books
3. abortive attempts
4. gestalt
5. successive approximation
6. ritual
7. steal from the best
8. audience
9. abandonment

Lichtenbergian Press

ISBN 978-1-7334670-4
520

www.ingramcontent.com/pod-product-compliance
Lightning Source LLC
Chambersburg PA
CBHW061738070526
44585CB00024B/2725